THE
usher's
MANUAL

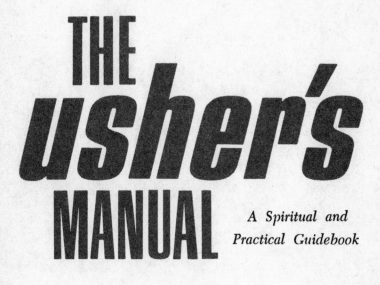

THE usher's MANUAL

A Spiritual and Practical Guidebook

by
LESLIE PARROTT

ZONDERVAN
PUBLISHING HOUSE
OF THE ZONDERVAN CORPORATION
GRAND RAPIDS, MICHIGAN 49506

THE USHER'S MANUAL
Copyright © 1970 by Zondervan Publishing House
Grand Rapids, Michigan

ISBN 0-310-30651-5

Library of Congress Catalog Card Number 72-95041

Printed in the United States of America

83   84   85   86   87   88 — 30   29   28   27   26   25   24   23

AN INTRODUCTION

Ushering has been a step-child in many churches for too long. The usher is a personal representative of Jesus Christ who meets people on a person-to-person basis when they first arrive at church. As such, the usher's ministry of service must be accepted and recognized as an important one.

In many smaller churches, these step-children called "ushers" are kept from sight most of the time, at least until collection time, and then they fade from sight again. Morale among ushers is low, and there is little feeling of being needed, or belonging.

In other churches the enthusiasm of the ushers and greeters is contagious. Their skills have been developed and their attitudes are good because they have accepted the challenge of a person-to-person ministry in the church and are striving for a high standard of excellence which they know the pastor and people have come to expect. In these churches the ushers are brought into the planning and communications on an equal level with the choir and the Sunday school teachers. The head usher is chosen with the same care traditionally used in selecting Sunday school superintendents and youth leaders. The silent ministry of these efficient, people-oriented ushers is a blessing to every church service.

Every church can have an effective group of ushers. This *Usher's Manual* is intended as a guide to reaching this goal. Begin by reading the guidelines on "How To Use This Manual." Then continue the study of the chapters as a reference book and a training tool for developing the ministry of ushering in the church.

Many ideas in this *Usher's Manual* have come from my observance of the outstanding ministry performed by the board of ushers in the church where I pastor. The longtime chairman of this group is Mr. Clarence Freeburg, who is the best head usher I ever have known.

— LESLIE PARROT

Portland, Oregon
January 1, 1970

HOW TO USE THIS MANUAL

The Usher's Manual is planned to fill three needs in the church: First, it is hoped that pastors, ushers, and congregations will see the high importance of ushering and be motivated to lift the standard of excellence among ushers to the level of a "ministry" in local churches.

Second, the complete index and scope of questions discussed in this manual are intended to make it more useful as a reference tool. No two church ushering situations are alike. Solutions to ushering problems offered in this manual may be totally inept in some situations. This manual is not intended as an arbitrary authority but as a point of reference. All policies and solutions to specific ushering problems must be worked out on the basis of common sense in the local situation. Taken as a guide, this manual can be a useful tool for reference in these matters.

Third, *The Usher's Manual* is intended to be a training tool for pastors and head ushers to use in local churches. Each man on the Board of Ushers in a local church should own his own copy. It should be read, studied in ushers' meetings, and used for training drills. Suggestions for discussion and training exercises are included at the end of each chapter.

These five chapters may be used for five training sessions as follows:

Chapter 1, on "The Ministry of Ushering," is intended to help inspire and motivate ushers in making their work a ministry, not a job, in the church. The pastor is the best person to present this material and to inspire the men to a new level of usefulness. The Usher's Prayer at the close of the chapter may be read in unison by the men at the close of the session. The Usher's Commission may be used by the pastor in a public installation service for the ushers.

Chapter 2, on "The Functions of an Usher," deals with the attitudes of an usher toward people, toward the service in progress, and toward himself. These attitudes are more important than many suspect in determining the final quality of service rendered by an usher. The second half of the chapter deals with the techniques of ushering as they relate to the people and to the church service. Use of this chapter should involve (1) a consultation with the pastor, (2) a study of the church bulletin and usual format of the services, and (3) actual practice in the sanctuary.

Chapter 3, on "An Usher's Standard of Excellence," may be used in a discussion session. Assign several men to discuss the main points under paragraph #80 on "A More Excellent Way." Follow their remarks with a discussion period. Follow the same technique with paragraph #81 on "A Sense of the Fitness of Things." These presentations and discussions will be useful and productive to the degree they are directly related to the specific attitudes, techniques, and problems of ushers in your church.

Chapter 4, on "The Authority and Responsibility of Ushers," is very important in the administration of an ushering ministry. A panel presentation may be made by (1) the pastor, (2) the lay leader of the church board, and (3) the head usher. This session would be a good time to bring in the Sunday school superintendent, the choir director, the organist and pianist. If there is a separate Greeters Committee in the church besides the ushers, the chairman of this group should be invited also. To clarify the issues in this chapter, there will need to be questions asked by the group and answered by the men on the panel.

Chapter 5, on "The Ushers As Greeters," may be a training session. Suggestions are made at the end of the chapter on how to demonstrate and train men in the techniques of (1) remembering names, and (2) introducing new people.

To aid in study and discussion, the paragraphs in *The Usher's Manual* are numbered for ready reference.

TABLE OF CONTENTS

CHAPTER 4

CHAPTER 5

1

THE MINISTRY OF USHERING

Preaching, teaching, music and ushering

1. Any act of Christian service which helps direct men into fellowship with Jesus Christ is a ministry. The most prominent ministry in the church is *preaching*. Although St. Paul referred to it as "the foolishness of preaching," he also wrote to the Romans, "How shall they believe in him of whom they have not heard? And how shall they hear without a preacher?" (Romans 10:14). Even in churches which have set the pulpit to one side and have made the altar the center of worship, preaching still is the most prominent part of the service. Other churches have made the pulpit the center of worship by the prominence of the sermon in the service and by the central placement of the pulpit on the platform.

2. The second prominent ministry in the church is *teaching*. Next to the preaching of the Gospel, Martin Luther believed teaching was the highest calling of mankind. Teaching is mentioned many times in the New Testament and included among the spiritual gifts. The pastor who preaches without teaching, or the church which evangelizes without instructing is not only obscuring the cross of Christ but failing to provide the Holy Spirit with opportunity for one of His most important functions; "He shall teach you all things, and bring all things to your remembrance, whatsoever I have said unto you" (John 14:26). "He will guide you into all truth" (John 16:13). In one of his letters to Timothy, St.

11

Paul said, "The servant of the Lord must . . . be gentle unto all men, *apt to teach*, patient; in meekness *instructing those* that oppose themselves" (II Timothy 2:24, 25).

3. The third great ministry in the church is *music*. According to St. Paul, music is at least on an equal plane with teaching as a ministry in the church: "Let the word of Christ dwell in you richly . . . teaching and admonishing one another in psalms and hymns and spiritual songs" (Colossians 3:16). The importance of the Holy Spirit in the ministry of music was further emphasized by St. Paul in his correspondence with the Corinthians: "I will sing with the Spirit and I will sing with the understanding also."

4. The fourth great ministry of the church is ushering. St. Paul who believed in the power of preaching, the importance of teaching, and the ministry of music, also wrote, "Let all things be done decently and in order" (I Corinthians 14:40). The importance of the usher's ministry caused one pastor to say, "If I had to choose between losing the ushers or the choir, I would rather lose the choir." This probably was an exaggeration used to emphasize the importance of the ministry of ushering in his church. But it is a fact that it will take music from a very extraordinary choir to overcome the poor work of inefficient ushers. In fact, it probably is true that all four of these ministries interact on a fairly equal basis in any given local church. Though of unequal importance, preaching, teaching, singing, and ushering are also closely related to each other that one does not tend to rise above the other in a given church. The preachers, teachers, musicians, and ushers, all need each other!

Ushering in the Old Testament

5. Ushers in the Old Testament tabernacle, and later in the temple, were called doorkeepers. The Psalmist, who wrote to the chief musician in the temple, understood the importance of ushers when he said, "How amiable are thy tabernacles, O Lord of Hosts! . . . Blessed are they that dwell in thy house: they will be still praising thee. . . . I had rather be *a doorkeeper in the house of my God,* than to dwell

"We all need each other"

"A doorkeeper in the house of the Lord is no small thing!"

in the tents of wickedness" (Psalm 84:1, 4, 10). One of the functions of doorkeepers in the Old Testament was to receive the collections from the people: "Go up to Hilkiah the high priest, that he may sum the silver which is brought into the house of the Lord, which *the keepers of the door* have gathered from the people" (II Kings 22:4). Jeremiah refers to one of these doorkeepers as a "man of God." He said, "And I brought them into the house of the Lord, into the chamber of the sons of Hanan . . . a man of God . . . *the keeper of the door*" (Jeremiah 35:4). The Old Testament Chronicler wrote of Shallum and his brethren who "were over the work of the service, *keepers of the gates of the tabernacle . . . keepers of the entry*" (I Chronicles 9:19).

6. The preacher in Ecclesiastes wrote about "the day when the *keepers of the house* shall tremble" (Ecclesiastes 12:3). And in Ezekiel's version of a future temple, he saw space reserved for the priests, the musicians, and two sets of ushers: "The *keepers of the charge of the house*," and "the *keepers of the charge of the altar*" (Ezekiel 40:45, 46).

Ushers in the New Testament

7. In the New Testament, the temple ushers were given unusual authority, evidently as uniformed guards. In the Acts of the Apostles, "the captain of the temple" and "the officers" are referred to several times in connection with arrests and general handling of the crowds. It was these doorkeepers or ushers, who carried out the orders of the high priests in the persecutions in the temple against the Apostles immediately following Pentecost, and 30 years later in the arrests and maltreatment of St. Paul.

8. Jesus used His disciples for the functions of ushers on many occasions. They prepared the way for His coming, they introduced people to Him, and in general directed the people who had come to hear Him speak or to be touched by His healing hands. On one occasion, Jesus gave a sharp warning to the disciples, who as ushers had endeavored to keep children away from the Master. On still another occasion, Jesus directed the disciples in organizing a congrega-

"Men of honest report, full of faith
and wisdom and of the Holy Spirit"

tion of 5,000 men plus women and children, to be seated in groups of 50. Then, with Christ supplying the unending loaves and fishes, the disciples served the hungry multitude.

9. It was among the functions of the first church board to serve as ushers: "Then the twelve called the multitude of the disciples unto them, and said, It is not reason that we should leave the Word of God, and serve tables. Wherefore, brethren, look ye out among you seven men . . . whom we may appoint over this business. But we will give ourselves continually to prayer, and to the ministry of the word. And the saying pleased the whole multitude" (Acts 6:2-5). The character of these first deacons is spelled out clearly: They were (a) men of honest report, (b) men full of the Holy Ghost, (c) men full of wisdom, and (d) men full of faith. This means then that Stephen the first Christian martyr on record, was both a member of the church board and served tables daily as an usher or deacon.

What makes a good usher

10. The three qualities of good men explained by Jesus in the Sermon on the Mount could not be more applicable than they are to the ministry of church ushers: First, the ministry of ushering is like salt which makes everything more palatable and which serves as a general preservative against deterioration. Jesus did not say, "*Ye ought* to be the salt of the earth," but He said, "*Ye are*" (Matthew 5:13). Ushers enjoy the ministry of a constructive influence. Paul said, "Let your speech be always with grace, seasoned with salt" (Colossians 4:6). A good usher adds a tang of joy to a churchgoer's Sunday morning experience instead of a tinge of drabness. Also, the ministry of an usher is like salt because salt can never do its work until it is brought into close contact with the substance on which it is to make its influence. The church ushers, pastors, musicians, or teachers, come into direct contact on an individual basis with more people in a given service than anyone else who ministers to them. The ministry of salt is silent, inconspicuous, and

"How is an usher like salt —
     a city on a hill —
          and a lamp stand?"

sometimes completely unnoticed. But it is there — in a powerful and useful way.

11. Also, a good usher is like "a city set upon a hill" (Matthew 5:14). While ushers are like inconspicuous salt, they also may become like a city on a hill. They become landmarks to churchgoers who learn to depend upon them. Stability helps overcome many other weaknesses in the priority of qualifications among ushers. The first glimpse of an usher on whom a churchgoer has come to depend brings an internal sense of welcome repose; someone is on hand who is interested in me! It is not uncommon for an usher to become an advisor, a source of information, counselor, or better yet, an intermediary between the needs of a specific person and the resources available through the pastor, musicians, and teachers of the church.

12. Third, a good usher is like a lamp on a stand, not put "under a bushel but on a candlestick; and it giveth light unto all that are in the house" (Matthew 5:15). A lamp brings warmth and welcome to all who are in the room. One flickering candle can brighten the conversation in a room and bring an inner feeling of warmth and joy. As a lamp dispels the darkness and brings emotional warmth to a room, so the ministry of an usher can make a similar intangible contribution to all who experience the inner light of pleasure in people which he allows to shine through himself. Jesus concluded this discussion on the character of a good usher by saying, "Let your light so shine before men, that they may see your good works, and glorify your Father which is in heaven" (Matthew 5:16). It is the nature of Christian character to radiate; it cannot help but shine. But the radiance of this glory is not for "self" but for the Kingdom of God. The ministry of an usher is not intended to bring glory to himself but to God. Just as a pastor preaches in the Spirit, and a musician sings in the Spirit, the usher must do his work in the power of the Holy Spirit — bringing glory to God in the Lord's house on the Lord's day.

Why ushers are so important

13. One day, in Chicago, Illinois, Mr. Wrigley looked mournfully down upon the streams of customers who stood before the ticket boxes at Wrigley field to get refunds for the baseball seats which they had bought but could not locate. While Mr. Wrigley groaned inwardly about the loss of his customers, Andy Frain, a young man in his early twenties, approached the financial wizard and begged for the job of head usher at the great baseball stadium. Destitute for a solution to his problems, Wrigley hired him.

14. In only a few years Andy Frain completely revolutionized ushering at Wrigley Field and made himself "King of the Ushers." Even more important, he made ushering a respectable new vocation. Mr. Frain organized a school for his men whom he had hand picked from many applicants. He gave them blackboard drills and showed them training films. At the completion of their training each recruit passed a test and was interned for two weeks of field work before receiving a diploma complete with a blue uniform, brass buttons, and gold stripes.

15. In a few years, Andy Frain had expanded his ushering to include many of the great auditoriums and arenas in the United States. In a single year his ushers handled crowds equal to the entire population of the United States. Through his branch offices in every major American city, Mr. Frain supervised every large gathering in the nation. Even the Democrats and Republicans agreed on one thing, Andy Frain's ushers would handle the crowds at both National conventions.

16. While the need for good ushers has been recognized and met in the large secular auditoriums, the need for good ushers is being recognized more and more by the leading clergymen. Even two generations ago, Dwight L. Moody was particular about his ushers and personally hired the 500 men who were to seat the crowds for the revival meeting he held in New York City. In current city-wide revivals no little attention is given to the need for efficient ushering.

Large crews of volunteer men are recruited and trained in advance to contribute no small part of both the seating of the people and the smooth operation of the invitation. But in churches, small and large, clergymen more and more are relying upon efficient ushers for smoothness in handling the individual problems which relate to the congregation. There are four reasons why the importance of the ministry of ushering has been recognized more and more:

17. To begin with, the usher is often the first official representative of Jesus Christ seen by people entering God's house. Teachers meet the people in the religious education classroom. Pastors face the people from behind a protecting pulpit after everyone is assembled in his place. Choir members sing with their eyes fastened on the director, not the people. But before members of the congregation ever see the pastor, the musicians, or even the teachers, they come face to face with a church usher. The attitude which the usher communicates to church members and friends helps set the spiritual tone for everything else which is to happen. As an official representative of the church and of Jesus Christ, the usher has an enormous obligation in helping lead people into readiness for learning, worshiping, and evangelism.

18. Second, the church usher may be the only individual contact the church makes directly with persons during their attendance in a service. Preachers, teachers and musicians minister to people in groups while ushers only minister to people as individuals. A Spirit-directed word of encouragement, reassurance, or kindness may be the most significant ministry some people receive in their entire church attendance experience. Only a few can linger to meet the pastor, to ask questions of the teachers, and to talk with the musicians; but everyone may have a first-hand encounter with the ministry of a good usher.

19. Third, the usher is the only person whose functions cannot be replaced or omitted. Preaching in a given service has been omitted. There have been services without choirs; and on occasion classes have been dismissed. But there is no substitute for the work of ushers in any church service re-

gardless of its character. In weddings, funerals, communion services, evangelistic campaigns, patriotic rallies, cantatas, Christmas plays, films, and any other kind of church meeting, ushers are important.

20. Finally, an usher is a forerunner. As John the Baptist was a forerunner for the ministry of Jesus Christ, the church usher is a forerunner for all the other ministries in the congregation. An attitude the usher demonstrates in the foyer of the church is a forerunner of the ministry to be experienced in the sanctuary. An usher in the vestibule can enhance or detract from the ministry in the channel by the way he administers his own duties.

An usher's prayer

21. "May I, dear Lord, in church today, fulfill my assignment in a Christ-like way. Make me efficient in what I do, effective in what I say, understanding by the way I feel about people, and helpful in the attitudes I have toward them. Make me a co-worker with the pastor, the church musicians, the teachers, and most of all, Lord, with Thee. Save me from hurtful words and harmful deeds. Make people glad they came to our church today because the Holy Spirit ministered to their needs through the sermons and prayers of the pastor, through the music of the organist and singers, through the explanations of understanding teachers, and through the ministry of ushers like me. In Christ's Name, Amen."

An usher's commission

22. "At the beginning of another year the church gives you this fresh commission, new and yet old. Allow the hospitality of this church to become incarnate in you. Wrap every word and clothe every action in the spirit of human kindness. May your kind of Christianity help people to let down their guards, open their hearts, and relax their minds for the worship of God and direction of His Holy Spirit. Be understanding with the difficult person. Exercise compassion with all kinds of people. Learn to be efficient, but

not at the expense of kindness. And accept from the pastor and congregation this assignment which ranks in importance with the other ministries of this church. May your highest good be the kindness of human understanding, your greatest virtue the stability of a man in Christ, and your most effective tool, the indwelling presence of the Holy Spirit who is the Spirit of Christ."

SUGGESTIONS FOR STUDY AND TRAINING

1. The purpose of this chapter is to help the ushers to see the prime importance of their assignment as a ministry for Jesus Christ and His church.

2. In a training session, this chapter may be presented by the pastor or other qualified person held in respect by the men. The speaker should be a person who is able to motivate others.

3. Assign persons to read the Old Testament Scripture references on ushering as an opening devotional for the meeting. They are as follows:

Psalm 81:1, 4, 10
II Kings 22:4
Jeremiah 35:4
I Chronicles 9:19
Ezekiel 40:45, 46

4. Questions for discussion:
   a) In what way is the work of an usher like salt?
   b) What church ushers have you known who became real person-to-person ministers as ushers? Tell about them.
   c) In what ways can the presence of a good usher be like a lamp which gives emotional warmth to a church?
   d) What is the worst ushering situation you have experienced?

5. Using a blackboard, ask the men to identify all the problems they think of concerning ushering in your local church. Write all these on the board and if pos-

sible have a list mimeographed for later use in other training sessions.

6. Close the session with everyone reading "The Usher's Prayer" in unison.

2

THE FUNCTIONS OF AN USHER

23. The unpardonable sin of a church usher is inattention. Signals are missed, communications are not heard, the needs of people are ignored, and the quality of an usher's effectiveness drops to zero when his mind wanders. The admonition of St. Paul includes ushers when he said, "And whatsoever ye do, do it heartily, as to the Lord . . . for ye serve the Lord Christ" (Colossians 3:23, 24). No less concentration is needed by the usher than is necessary for the pastor, organist, pianist, choir director, soloist, or teacher. The usher is there to serve the people with individual help. In this ministry there are three areas of concentration:

24. *Concentrate on the people.* Since the seating habits of people tend to be established, learn these arrangements. Prompt, direct seating of people in their usual place is an indication to them of the usher's awareness. Seating visitors next to regular churchgoers with a word of introduction is helpful to new people. Awareness of empty seats in this general seating pattern comes only by concentration. If ushers were ranked like men in the army, a promotion should be given to every usher who learns to concentrate on people's names.

25. *Concentrate on the service.* It is possible for a church usher to concentrate both on the people he is serving and on the church service in progress. Since every part of a Sunday morning worship service makes its own contribution to the total worship experience, it is good for the usher to

know what is going on at a given moment and why this has been planned:

26. (a) Worship begins with reverent quietness. During the last moments before the service begins, many congregations sit in quiet reverence, relaxing their minds and bodies while they meditate. In these precious moments of quietness while the organ is playing, devout Christians have opportunity to pray, think, and read their Bibles. Everything an usher does in these moments should help contribute to this atmosphere.

27. (b) Call to worship. A choral call to worship by the choir or a spoken invocation and admonition by the pastor helps bring the congregation to attention and directs their thoughts to God. No person should be seated during the call to worship.

28. (c) Congregational singing. Beginning with the Protestant reformation, hymn-singing has become a most important means for praise and worship. Since the congregation often stands for singing, this is one of the best times for seating latecomers.

29. (d) Scripture reading. It is an indication of thoughtless irreverence to seat worshipers during the reading of the Bible. The usher may stop people from being seated and may himself concentrate on the reading of the Scripture by standing firmly at the head of the aisle during the reading of the Bible.

30. (e) The pastoral prayer. Nothing done in the morning service is more important than the pastor's prayer for the people. Representing every worshiper in the service, the pastor lifts his voice in praise and petition during some of the most sacred moments of the service. This is not the time for ushers to check the heat or run errands. It is to their spiritual advantage to participate in this prayer.

31. (f) The ministry of music. Anthems, gospel songs, choral arrangements, solos, and ensembles are used for a special ministry in music. No one is seated during these moments because of the distraction to both the singers and listeners.

An ill-groomed usher, "Never in our church!"

32. (g) Offertory. By the time the offering is received, most latecomers already have been seated. The offering is a means of worship and expresses the congregation's most tangible indication of commitment.

33. (h) Moments of meditation. After the pastor has read his text or announced the theme of his message, many congregations are asked to bow their heads in quiet thought. This not only serves to help prepare them for the sermon but also gives opportunity for them to hear the voice of the Holy Spirit. Everyone, including ushers, should be still.

34. (i) Sermon. Although the duties of ushers continue through the entire service, it is good for them to participate in the message by active listening.

35. (j) Invitation hymn. An attitude of prayerful attention on the part of the ushers is a help to the invitation. Also, they may assist persons to "come forward" for prayer. In some churches the ushers have received instruction in personal work.

36. (k) Final benediction. The last act of worship in most services is a prayer of divine blessing on the people as they leave the sanctuary. The final amen in this prayer is a cue to the ushers for all doors to be opened and preparations made for helping the people leave the church.

37. The church usher who concentrates on what is happening in the service and why, will do a more effective job and will receive more personal help from the service for himself. Ushering does not require men to be detached from, or immune to, the means of grace.

38. *Concentrate on yourself.* Self-centered conceit is repulsive, but self-assurance and self-respect are admired. The usher who concentrates on the people and the church service, will find it easy to concentrate on his own relationship to both of them. Here is a church usher's checklist on himself.

39. *His grooming.*

—— Personal cleanliness
—— Deodorant
—— Mouthwash

—— No chewing gum
—— Hair groomed
—— Clean shaven
—— Suit pressed
—— Shoes shined
—— Clean shirt and tie
—— Never remove suitcoat

40. *His assignment.*

—— On time
—— Never leave post
—— Do not assume authority
—— Concentrate on the service
—— Concentrate on the service
—— Special attention to guests
—— Adequate supply of envelopes, hymn books, and bulletins
—— Follow instructions

41. *His attitude.*

—— Proud to be an usher
—— Optimistic about *our* church
—— Pleasant conversation
—— Pleasant face
—— Non-judgmental attitude
—— Prayerful

An ambassador of kindness

42. Since the contacts of an usher are made directly with the people as individuals, it is important that he learn to think with kindness and understanding about persons. Do not expect too much from people. An effective usher learns how to accept people as they are instead of the way he wishes they were. For instance; since it is the nature of teenagers to be thoughtless, fickle, detached, bored, and even rebellious, the usher will not help the teenagers or the church's ministry by thinking unkind thoughts about them. Allowing teens and children to be true to their nature without censure or criticism may be more helpful than a whole lecture on the "oughts."

43. Another special group in the church is the older people. They need more reassurance than young adults with growing families. Awareness of their special needs — seeing and hearing problems — may be like the cup of cold water given in His Name.

44. Perhaps the most needy people in a given church service are first time visitors. Many deplorable stories have been told about the encounters of new people with church ushers. It does not take much effort to say, "Hello." A smiling welcome — "We like our church very much and we hope you will enjoy the service today" — may be as reassuring to a church visitor as a lifeline to a man in deep water. Identification of cloak rooms, rest rooms, and a word of introduction to one or two church members may be the difference between anxiety and happy adjustment with the new visitor.

45. Kindness in conversation can be developed among ushers who try. Negative statements which tend to be judgmental and smack of criticism are the very opposite of kindness. Here are some examples:

46. Negative: "You cannot go in now!"
Positive: "We will seat you in just a moment."

47. Negative: "You're late; you'll have to sit in the back!"
Positive: "Since the service has started, we have a place for you near the back."

48. Negative: "You can't stand here in everybody's way!"
Positive: "Would you like to visit over here where people will not interfere with your conversation?"

49. Negative: "At your age, I suppose you need a hearing aid!"
Positive: "We have some good seats up front where everyone can see and hear the best."

50. Negative: "You teen-agers shut up!"
Positive: "Will you young people help us promote reverence in the sanctuary?"

51. There is one final word of warning about expressing kindness: Ushers should be careful not to place their hands

on people in either persuasion or familiarity. Let kindness come from the heart instead of the hands!

Seating the people

52. The foremost of an usher's two major functions is to seat the people. This is how people are seated:

53. First, the ushers should arrive perhaps 30 minutes before service time to receive their door and aisle assignments from the head usher. After surveying the section to be sure that envelopes, hymnbooks, Bibles, pencils, and other materials are in the racks, the usher takes his supply of church bulletins and begins seating responsibilities with the arrival of the first worshiper. This aisle assignment continues until the end of the service even though the usher may be seated after the offering has been received.

54. Second, the ushers will seat people as near the front and center as seems appropriate. Back seats always can be filled with people coming in later, but it is often difficult to secure the cooperation of latecomers in being seated down front. It is the poorest technique to seat the sanctuary from the back to the front. Many churches use rope devices in reserving the last three pews in the sanctuary for latecomers. However, if someone insists in being seated near the back, it is better to have them in the rear than not to have them at all.

55. Third, when persons arrive at the head of the aisle to be seated, the usher will give them a friendly recognition and then suggest his plan for seating them. For instance, he may say, "I would like to seat you about halfway down." Or, "I have two seats on the aisle." "I believe you will enjoy the service more if you are seated near the front." People tend to respond with cooperation to a suggestion. However, if an usher falls into the trap of asking people, "Where would you like to be seated?" he is in trouble. This may throw them into the same kind of dilemma some people face in trying to choose from a menu.

56. Fourth, the usher will walk slowly down the aisle

stopping at the pew where the people are to be seated and forming a little gate into the seating area by placing his hand on the back of the pew in front. If the usher walks too fast, people will lag behind and feel very much alone. They even may slip into a seat nearer the back and leave the usher standing with no one to seat. There is dignity in walking slowly, and the people are close enough behind to whisper a question or word of instruction to the usher if need be. In all cases, the usher does not give a church bulletin to the worshiper until after he is seated. This keeps him "in charge" even if the people have deserted his place for a seat of their own.

57. Fifth, there are two basic rules in seating the congregation: (1) The usher never allows any diversion to keep him from being aware of the people who arrive at the head of his aisle for seating. He never leaves his station or lapses into inattention. (2) An usher never points to a seat and sends people off down the aisle by themselves. He shows them to their seats, personally.

58. Sixth, there are several ways to be sure an usher is on hand at the head of the aisle at all times for seating people. In large churches with long aisles, two ushers to an aisle may be necessary. In these instances an usher sometimes stands at the head of the aisle greeting the people and then directing them to another usher who is halfway down the aisle, ready to seat them. In other churches, a roving usher is stationed halfway between two aisles and steps to the assistance of his colleagues whenever needed. This roving usher actually works in two aisles of the church. In smaller churches, one usher per aisle is all that is needed.

The church offering

59. At least since the days of St. Paul, taking a collection in church has been a regular part of worship: "Now concerning the collection . . . upon the first day of the week let every one of you lay by him in store, as God hath pros-

"There are some seats over there"

pered him" (I Corinthians 16:1, 2). The church offering consists of the following five factors:

60. *First is the processional:* In most churches, the ushers who seat the people receive the offering in their same aisle. However, some churches do use a separate set of ushers who are seated on the very front pew, ready for their assignment when the offering time comes. Ordinarily, the pastor will use some introductory remarks or Scripture passage to prepare the minds of the people for giving. Then on a signal given by the head usher, or the pastor, the processional of ushers begins. With a little practice, the ushers can walk in step and keep abreast as they proceed from the rear of the sanctuary to the front. Precision in this procedure is the mark of good discipline among ushers.

61. *Second is the distribution of the offering plates:* In some churches the head usher distributes offering plates to the men in the rear of the sanctuary and they carry the plates under their right arms as they proceed to the front. In other churches, the offering plates are on the communion table as symbols of worship and are distributed by the pastor or lay officer in the church.

62. *Third is the blessing or dedication:* If ushers bring offering plates with them to the front of the sanctuary, they usually stop in line with the first pew. If a prayer of blessing and thanksgiving is prayed before the offering is received, the ushers stand reverently in their places until the pastor has concluded the prayer. If the offering plates are distributed from the communion table, then the ushers must proceed to the front and center of the sanctuary to receive their plates and wait reverently for the prayer of blessing. As a third alternative, some churches instruct their ushers to bring their offering plates with them from the rear of the sanctuary and to proceed immediately to receive the offering beginning with the first pew and working back to the rear. After the offering is received, the plates are given to two ushers who bring them down the center aisle to stand before the communion table where a prayer of dedication is

offered by the pastor. The offering then is placed on the
communion table until the service is over. The return of the
ushers to the front of the sanctuary is often accompanied
by the congregation who stand to sing "The Doxology." If
the pastor prefers to pray for the offering before it is received, then the offering plates are turned over to the **head**
usher or other church officials who have authority for counting and depositing the funds. Informal, haphazard ushering
during the offering is an indication of an unplanned service
and a failure to perceive giving as a means of grace.

63. *Fourth is the actual receiving of the collection.* Here
again there is room for variety of procedure. Ordinarily
there is one usher to an aisle who works pews on both sides
of the aisle at the same time. Only in churches with special
seating problems should the offering plates be handed back
by the worshipers from one pew to another. If on occasion
an offering plate is dropped by a worshiper, it is the job
of the head usher or special usher to retrieve the funds and
handle the emergency while the regular ushers proceed with
their collection assignment.

64. *Fifth is the offertory.* Regardless of the procedures
used in the processional, the prayer, distribution of the
plates, and the actual collection, the offertory is a means of
grace and should be heard out to its conclusion. Background
music is for elevators and dining rooms, but an offertory is
a ministry of music.

Miscellaneous functions

65. Besides the major duties of the usher in seating people
and receiving the collection, there are many other smaller
functions of vital importance. Here are a few:

66. *Hearing aids.* The ushers have authority and responsibility in the distribution and use of hearing aids among
those who need them. This means knowledge of equipment,
ample space for storage and alertness in making the equipment available.

"You may sit with me until service is over"

67. *Children who leave the service:* Children should learn very early that it is not permissible to wander in and out from the front seats of the sanctuary. This is especially true if the children come from non-church homes and are seated apart from supervising adults. Ushers must treat these children very kindly but they cannot be allowed to disturb the service. Either seat wandering children in the back or provide them with special chairs in the foyer so they will not disturb other worshipers by returning to their seats. Also, when one child leaves the service it tends to start a procession of others. Appropriateness and understanding are necessary in handling this rather delicate problem. But with tact and kindness children can learn to stay in the sanctuary throughout the entire service. People with special physical problems which make it necessary for them to leave the service should be seated near the rear.

68. *Seating of latecomers:* Latecomers should be seated during the singing of the hymns, but never during the reading of Scripture or during the ministry of special music. Very latecomers who arrive after the sermon has begun, should be seated as inconspicuously as possible. Reserved back seats have been a big help in alleviating this problem in many churches.

69. *Registering of guests:* In many churches the ushers are wholly or partially responsible for the registering of guests. Although the system and techniques must be worked out in detail with the pastor and head usher, procedures must include means for identifying guests on sight, making registration materials available to the guests, and turning the results over to the pastor or church office. Many churches use cards while others use guest books. Some use both. The important thing is to make a guest feel welcome. Some guests do not want to be identified; and in this case their privacy should be respected.

70. *Handling of "characters":* Drunks, panhandlers, and other types of characters sometimes drift into churches expecting to reap the benefits of Christian humanitarianism.

These situations must be handled with Christian kindness, but firmness, without involving the pastor. Most city churches, who have a greater share of this kind of problem, have procedures already outlined and in the possession of ushers.

71. *Emergency procedures:* Physical sickness, fire, power failure, and other emergency procedures should be planned in advance. The telephone numbers for the police department, fire department, public utilities, ambulance service, and physicians' service should be readily available. Fire extinguishers, flashlights, candles, and matches should be on hand. And even more important are the procedures worked out in advance by the ushers.

72. *Parking problems:* The larger the church the greater the problems of parking. Commercial procedures for providing parking facilities in close proximity to shopping areas have now become the pattern for churches. In some churches it is now the responsibility of ushers to help people with their parking problems. White, three-quarter length coats, or other indentifying apparel, are worn by ushers who park cars for people, or assist drivers in the best use of the nearest parking facilities to the church. In some instances the same men double as traffic control officers when parking lots face on busy streets or highways.

73. *Communion services:* In some churches, ushers participate in the distribution of the elements in communion services. In general, the same techniques are used as in receiving the collection. However, in serving communion, twice as many men are needed because of the double distribution of bread and wine. Details for this service should be worked out completely between the pastor and head usher. Many churches make charts of their seating arrangements and assign men to specific row responsibilities. The goal in this distribution is to serve everyone as quickly as possible but in an atmosphere of devotional dignity.

74. *Keeping records:* Accurate records of attendance are considered the usher's responsibility in most churches. Mim-

eographed record forms are included among the ushers' supplies. An accurate record of attendance must be broken down to include all areas of the church where there are people. Besides the seating sections of the sanctuary, this record form should include the platform, choir, children's churches, nurseries, ushers on duty, and a miscellaneous item to cover persons in the hallways or on special assignment outside the sanctuary. The form also may include a place for a special note about weather or other conditions and circumstances affecting attendance. It is important to take this count in as inconspicuous a manner as possible. Some people resent being counted, and also, the process can become a distraction to the service.

75. *Weddings:* Although brides appoint their own ushers, it is good for the regular church ushers to be familiar with the procedure. Ordinarily the center aisle is not used for seating guests since this is reserved for the bride and her party. The aisle is sometimes covered with a white runner. Guests of the bride are seated on the left of the center aisle and guests of the bridegroom on the right. The parents of the bridegroom and the mother of the bride are seated on the same pew on opposite sides of the aisle. No one is ever seated in front of them. The last person to be seated before the wedding begins is the bride's mother. A very formal procedure is followed in seating guests at a wedding. Roving ushers ask the people as they arrive whether they are guests of the bride or groom, and then directs these guests to the proper aisle. The usher offers his arm to the lady while her escort follows them down the aisle to the place the usher has chosen for them to be seated. Since this is a slower process than ordinary church ushering, it is wise to have several men on duty to avoid a bottleneck at the head of the aisle. If guests say they have come in honor of both the bride and the groom, then they should be seated on the side of the aisle which has the least number of people. At the end of the wedding ceremony, everyone

remains seated until the ushers direct the people toward the exits, one pew at a time.

76. *Funerals:* Pallbearers ordinarily do not serve as ushers. Funerals held in mortuary chapels are usually ushered by the staff on duty. But in a church funeral, ushers often are needed for seating the mourners. Church funerals are often larger than those held in mortuary chapels. In many instances, a well-known person may have the tribute of an over-flow congregation at the funeral service. Quiet, efficient ushers will be needed under the general supervision of the mortician. He will pass on to the ushers any special information on seating arrangements desired by the family.

77. *Overflow congregations:* Special occasions such as Easter, Christmas, union services, and special denominational meetings often provoke attendances which overflow the main sanctuary. Dignity and preparedness on the part of the ushers will help to expedite all problems involved. If the plan for extra seats involves folding chairs, they should be readily available and placed in use by a pre-arranged plan. If balconies, foyers, and extra rooms are used for these occasions, the head usher should determine when each move is made to fill additional space. Also, lighting, heating and cooling, use of hymn books, amplified sound, and other needs should be thought through in advance. Informal conferences among ushers and disorganized scurrying about tend to be a distraction.

SUGGESTIONS FOR STUDY AND TRAINING

1. In the opening devotional assign one of the men to read and comment on the ushering Jesus needed for "Feeding the 5,000" (Matthew 14:13 - 23).

2. In consultation with the pastor, study the church bulletin for a better understanding of the order of service usually followed in your morning and evening services.

3. Consider with the pastor what could be done to increase reverence in the sanctuary and more smoothness of operation in the mechanics of the church service. Write down these suggestions on a blackboard.

4. Ask the pastor to explain the deeper meaning of the elements of worship indicated in paragraph #25.

5. Choose an appropriate person — man or woman — to discuss frankly the matters under paragraph #38. A panel of three persons could present the material in paragraphs #39, 40, and 41.

6. Ask two of the men to speak to an imaginary churchgoer on the following problems, one speaking kindly and the other abruptly and without kindness in tone of voice or words:

    a) Latecomer
    b) Offering plate dropped
    c) Slow moving
    d) Loud talking
    e) Crying baby
    f) Child leaving service

7. Go into the sanctuary and practice seating each other following the suggestions in paragraphs #52 through #58.

3

AN USHER'S STANDARD OF EXCELLENCE

The personality of a church

78. There is a difference in the personalities of churches just as there is among people. The three determinants of human personality are (1) the biological factors, (2) environmental factors, and (3) the inner self. This soul, or inner self, consists of attitudes, emotions and will. It is the self which interacts with the biological and environmental factors, making changes where possible, and constantly adjusting to the ongoing of life.

79. In a similar way the character and personality of a church depends on (1) physical factors, (2) environmental factors, and (3) the inner self. The physical factors include the church building with its capacities, limitations, and structural strengths and weaknesses. The environmental factors include the location of the church and its general setting in the community. In a church the inner self consists of its ministries — preaching, teaching, music, and ushering — and the combined attitudes, feelings, and wills of the people. In a church, the mind of Christ — who is the Holy Spirit — functions through the sum total of the people as they interact with each other, their environment, and the physical church building where they worship and work. The will of the people plus their attitudes and feelings will determine the standard of excellence at all levels in the church. Thus, everything which happens in the church including the janitorial service, noise level in the sanctuary, kind of church bulletin the people expect, pro-

Different Personalities?

cedures in the business of the church, congregational singing, special singing, preaching, teaching, religious education equipment, Sunday school facilities, and the quality of teaching and all else is a reflection of the standard of excellence in a particular church. Nowhere is this standard of excellence more obvious than in the ministry of ushering.

A more excellent way

80. After discussing the spiritual gifts at length, St. Paul said, ". . . and yet show I unto you a more excellent way" (I Corinthians 12:31). Paul then explained the importance of Christian love and detailed fifteen characteristics which apply to the ministry of ushering.

(1) "Charity suffereth long and is kind." There are many things in a church which an usher does not like. Part of his role is to absorb the criticisms people may not have a chance to give to other church officials. Some people, even among churchgoers, are difficult persons. But the test of excellence among church ushers is not their capacity to separate the good from the bad but to continue being kind under difficult circumstances.

(2) "Love envieth not." Personnel problems can become irksome even among church ushers. Inefficiency, bothersome little habits, or tendencies of other ushers to assume responsibility beyond their authority may create negative feelings within the board of ushers. Paul's only antidote for this is to accept each man as he is instead of how we wish he might be.

(3) "Love vaunteth not itself." A vaunting man makes a display of his own worth through boasting and bragging. This kind of usher concentrates more on the impression he is making than the people he is serving.

(4) "Love is not puffed up." A conceited, self-centered usher is below the standard of excellence for a spirit-filled church.

(5) "Love doth not behave itself unseemly." Regardless of the emergency, a good usher never loses his head. Stability and poise are characteristics of a high standard.

"Not easily provoked"

(6) "Love is not easily provoked." There are enough things happening in any given church to provoke the negative emotions of an usher. But the man with the high standard of excellence maintains an attitude of positive regard.

(7) "Love rejoiceth not in iniquity, but rejoiceth in the truth." Every church usher is either a part of the problem or a part of the solution. He is either more critical than helpful; or more helpful than critical. Stopping rumors, rejoicing in good reports, and always maintaining Christian optimism is a part of his standard of excellence.

(8) "Love beareth all things, believeth all things, hopeth all things, endureth all things." One of the differences between a good usher and a poor one is the capacity to deal effectively with problems. If there were no problems there would be no need for ushers; and yet some men become critical, irritated, and upset at the first irregularity in their assignment. The capacity to handle frustration, to make decisions quickly, and to work under pressure are qualities in an usher of excellence.

(9) "Love never faileth." One quality which eliminates stress in any kind of ushering emergency is human understanding. Value judgments, verbal explanations, excuses, and all other weapons used for handling emergencies are second best to an understanding heart.

(10) "And now abideth faith, hope, love, these three; but the greatest of these is love." An abiding faith, an optimistic outlook, and a love for God and people are all important in the standard of excellence set down by St. Paul. But of these three great qualities, the usher's highest good is his love of God which is reflected in his capacity to love people just as they are.

A sense of the fitness of things

81. This eternal sense of the fitness of things can never be legislated; "Against such there is no law" (Galatians 5:23). But a church usher who becomes a useful representative of Jesus Christ at the door of the sanctuary will seek for these

qualities of spirit which do not come by law but by the in-dwelling presence of the Holy Spirit:

(1) "The fruit of the Spirit is love." The New Testa-ment love St. Paul was writing about was an outgoing spirit of consideration and respect which did not depend on the attitudes or behavior of the other person. As one man put it, "The Holy Spirit can even help you love the person you do not like." This kind of love is not dependent on the other person's actions or reactions, but only on the attitudes of the one who loves. There never should be church strife in which an usher of high excellence is involved.

(2) "The fruit of the Spirit is joy." Cold, aloof. me-chanical ushering is depressing to churchgoers. But the sight of a good man who radiates joy as an effective usher is a heart-warming experience for any worshiper.

(3) "The fruit of the Spirit is peace." The presence of a good church usher adds to the peace and calm of every situation. His presence tends to minimize problems and his efficient way of dealing with situations is reassuring.

(4) "The fruit of the Spirit is longsuffering." Patience is one of the great qualities of a good usher. The church building itself, the environment around the church, the min-istry of the church, and the people in the congregation may all be occasions for impatience among ushers. But the long-suffering usher chooses the kinds of problems which he will allow to upset him.

(5) "The fruit of the Spirit is gentleness." Hallmarks of a Christian gentleman include thoughtfulness, keeping his hands to himself, acceptable language, and constant courtesy. The usher who has never developed the qualities of a gentle-man is loud, crude, jerky, and pawing.

(6) "The fruit of the Spirit is goodness." The Lord in His Word does not admonish men to be intelligent, clever, or rich. But He does in many places indicate that a basic quality of the Spirit-filled man is human goodness. Decep-tion in any of its forms is not compatible with Christian goodness.

(7) "The fruit of the Spirit is faith." Faith is used in several ways. There is saving faith, achieving faith, and doctrinal faith. There is faith in God, faith in people, and faith in one's self. The marginal reading indicates St. Paul in this instance meant achieving *faithfulness*. If so, he could not have been more accurate in describing a basic quality of excellence in a good usher. Being on time, and planning ahead concerning necessary absences are qualities of men who take their ministry of ushering seriously.

(8) "The fruit of the Spirit is meekness." No good usher ever throws around his authority. While he concentrates on the needs of the people he forgets about himself and humbly goes about his assignment.

(9) "The fruit of the Spirit is temperance." Christian temperance among good ushers manifests itself in a quality of cleanliness, good grooming, oral hygiene, and general demeanor. Since temperance can be applied to every relationship in life it is listed among St. Paul's highest qualities of Christian character.

(10) "Against such there is no law." No head usher or pastor can write enough rules to cover every situation which ushers face. Through a concentrated intelligence and a general sense of the fitness of things, ushers are called on to make unending little decisions which either become a part of the total church problem or its solution.

Sacred moments

82. Prayer, scripture reading, and the ministry of music are among the sacred moments in every church service. By their example of quiet attention, the ushers can help make these moments more meaningful to everyone. Movement in the building should be stopped, as much as possible, while all thoughts and actions are centered on talking with God, hearing from God through His Word, and receiving the ministry of music. The list of sacred moments in some churches may be enlarged to include other kinds of worship.

But with many, these three activities are more sacred than others.

Equipment and supplies

83. To be effective in their ministry, ushers need certain kinds of equipment and supplies which are readily available to them. The following list will serve as a starter:

(1) Ushers' desk and storage facility. Much like the bell captain in a hotel lobby, the head usher of a church needs a center of operation. It should be located in a convenient spot where people may come who have questions. It may contain the guest register, but it must contain storage space for all kinds of supplies used regularly by the ushers, including regular supplies as well as emergency equipment. This is the place for the intercom which connects the pastor with the ushers and possibly even the telephone for the congregation.

(2) First aid equipment. With half of the congregation consisting of children, there always is the possibility of accidents. Equipment for handling these emergencies should be in the possession of the head usher and stored in the ushers' desk.

(3) Identifying badges. In some churches ushers wear an identifying flower in their suit lapels. Others prefer an identifying badge. But in all instances ushers should be equipped with some identifying badge or symbol.

(4) Lost and found. The usher's central facility should contain room for lost and found items and should become the point for expediting these matters.

(5) Envelopes, guest cards, and writing materials. Each usher may be responsible for filling the racks on the backs of the pews of his section. Also, there are many times when writing materials, even for congregational distribution, are needed. These should be purchased in quantity and kept in storage by the head usher. Church offering envelopes, blank checks, and ball point pens are also needed among this equipment.

SUGGESTIONS FOR STUDY AND TRAINING

1. Assign one of the men to read Mark 10:13 - 16 in the opening devotional. Reflect on the importance of kindness to children.

2. Discuss frankly the personality of your church including the three factors of:
   a) physical property,
   b) community and regional environment, and
   c) the general attitudes of the congregation concerning your church.

3. Each man may be assigned a point of discussion under "A More Excellent Way," and also under "A Sense of the Fitness of Things."

4. The importance of the "Sacred Moments" may be discussed by a panel of three persons as outlined in paragraph #82.

4

THE AUTHORITY AND RESPONSIBILITY
OF USHERS

84. There are two factors in every administrative responsibility which cannot be separated; at least, not without losing a high degree of effectiveness. These two factors are authority and responsibility. If a man is given responsibility for a specific job but never the authority to implement it, the result is utter frustration. Also, if a man is the designated authority for a specific job but never given the responsibility, disorganization is the result. For ushers to do a good job in any local church, the areas of their responsibility and authority should be clearly understood. Ushers who assume authority beyond their responsibility create confusion, while ushers who do not accept the authority to fulfill their responsibility create ineffectiveness. Therefore, the following areas of authority and responsibility should be understood fully by the pastor, church board, head usher, ushers, and even the congregation.

The ultimate authority

85. In most churches the final authority for the operation of the church centers in the pastor and church board. But, since pastors and church boards cannot do everything which needs to be done, they delegate considerable authority and responsibility to laymen in the congregation. One of these areas of delegated authority and responsibility is church ushering. In matters of final decision the word of the pastor

or church board is ultimate. However, to facilitate matters, church boards and pastors usually appoint a head usher who is given responsibility and authority over ushering.

The head usher

86. The head usher needs to be a man of considerable maturity and Christian graces. He should be a person who feels comfortable about the pastor and the church. Since he may oversee the work of many men, he must be a person who works well with others. And since people often look with pride on the office of head usher, he should be an individual well accepted among the general population of the church. Once this man is chosen, he should be given full authority and responsibility for the church ushering job, referring back to the church board and pastor only on matters of policy.

(1) Recruitment. The head usher should have authority to recruit his own men. He will work best with men he has chosen. Even if there are men on the board of ushers whom he would not like to keep, the authority for his own decisions leaves him the full responsibility for his actions. He should not feel that certain ushers were handed to him without his consultation and accent. After studying the total situation he may decide to keep all the ushers from a previous year. But the decision should be his. Also, the head usher may want to choose more than one board of ushers. Some churches use a separate set of ushers for Sunday school, morning worship, and evening service. Still others rotate their ushers on a three months assignment basis. The head usher should not only decide on the men he will use but also the system for assigning their responsibilities.

(2) General supervision. Once the men have been recruited to serve as church ushers, it is the responsibility of the head usher to supervise all their functions. The head usher becomes the channel through whom the pastor works. Ushers with special problems do not take them direct to the pastor or board, but to the head usher. Unless the channels of communication are made crystal clear, the authority and

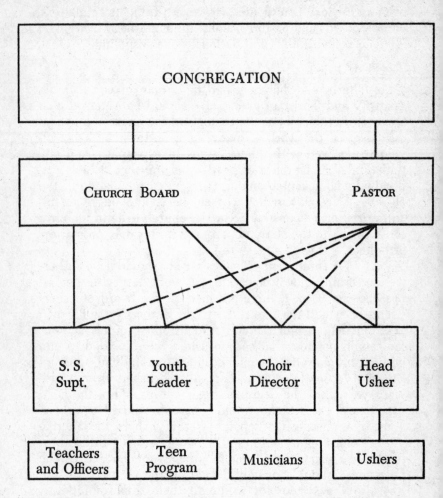

While working in consultation with the pastor, lay leaders must have both responsibility and authority for their assignments.

CHURCH GOVERNMENT: AUTHORITY AND RESPONSIBILITY

responsibility of the head usher in this regard will be thwarted. The pastor and others should not be giving instructions directly to ushers, but always through the head usher.

(3) Assignments. After studying his men, the head usher will make specific assignments to each man on his board of ushers. These may be annual assignments, or rotating assignments on the basis of the head usher's judgment. Any usher who cannot fulfill his assignment on a given day should make phone contact with the head usher as early as possible so a substitute may be recruited. In consultation with the pastor and the ushers, the head usher can determine how early men should arrive to begin their assignments. Rules and regulations governing the conduct and methods of the ushers should be worked out by the head usher in consultation with the men. Rules and regulations arbitrarily handed down by authority are often ineffective.

(4) Ushers meetings. Many head ushers meet with their men once each quarter for discussion on general and specific assignments. At least once each year it is good to make one of these gatherings a dinner meeting with the wives present. An usher may do a better job if his wife understands more fully his responsibility. And men always work together better when they have opportunity to break bread and discuss matters informally.

(5) Other duties. The head usher also has authority over the following areas: (a) attendance counting, (b) lost and found, (c) information center, (d) ordering supplies, and (e) liaison with the pastor during the service.

Individual ushers

87. Each individual usher has a right to know exactly what is required of him. He needs to know when he is to arrive. He must be trained in the techniques the head usher wants to use in seating the people and receiving the collections. He needs to know his specific aisle assignment and how long he is to stay at his post. If an individual usher reaches

"I'm sorry, Mr. New Family,
but I just don't know where the
junior department meets."

beyond his responsibility and authority, problems arise. Adjusting the heat, opening windows, closing doors, bringing in additional chairs, operating in another usher's aisle of responsibility, and passing unnecessary opinions are some of the ways ushers can create problems. But an usher who assumes the authority and fulfills the responsibility given him in a specific assignment is a man of God rendering a meaningful Christian service.

Know your church

88. Since ushers deal directly with individual churchgoers, it is necessary for them to know many things about their church which may not be necessarily understood by choir members or even Sunday school teachers. Ushers will be asked many questions which they can help answer if they are familiar with information on the following items:

1) Church office hours
2) Bus schedules
3) Rest room locations
4) Pastor's educational and professional background
5) The church manual or book of discipline
6) Church denominational headquarters
7) Parking
8) Publishing house addresses
9) In one of the usher's meetings, a blackboard may be used for listing the kinds of information the ushers are asked for most often about the church.

89. In all churches, but especially in larger ones, it is good for ushers to know well their local church building. Although this list should be made by each board of ushers, here are items which should be included:

1) The location of every Sunday school department and adult classroom.
2) The location of heating, plumbing, and electrical controls.
3) Checks should be made on all rest rooms (a) before Sunday school, (b) between Sunday school

and morning worship, (c) after the morning worship service, (d) before the evening service, and (e) after the evening service. Since many churches operate with minimum rest room facilities, deterioration can show up very quickly.

4) Location and policy on use of phones.
5) Church nursery facilities and policies.
6) The lost and found.
7) First aid facilities.

SUGGESTIONS FOR STUDY AND TRAINING

1. Assign one of the men to read St. Paul's admonition "concerning the collection" in I Corinthians 16:1 - 4.

2. Find a qualified person to give illustrations on the relationship of authority and responsibility.

3. Write on the board a list of the responsibilities of the head usher.

4. Write another list of the things an usher has a right to know about his assignment.

5. Make a diagram of your church showing locations for classes, materials, supplies, and heating and lighting controls.

THE USHERS AS GREETERS

90. There are two problems to face in the work of ushers as greeters. First, is the responsibility of ushering to be divided from assignment of greeters at the door? In some churches the responsibilities of church greeters and church ushers is divided. But even when special persons are designated for greeting the congregation as they arrive at the door, greeting is still at least a partial responsibility of every usher. Another problem relates to the plan the church has for greeting and ushering the congregation during the Sunday school hour. In some churches ushers do not assume their responsibilities until the close of Sunday school, while in others they are on duty from 30 minutes before Sunday school begins.

91. Ushers working between Sunday school and church have little opportunity for conversation with the people. Since large numbers of people are to be seated, the greeting generally must be confined to a nod, a smile, and a few quick words. Greeters meeting the people before Sunday school are often less cramped for time and therefore can visit more fully with new people. Some ushers are instructed to spot new people in their sections as they enter and during the service and then watch for an opportunity to welcome them more fully at the end of the service. There are several areas of consideration in greeting people:

"Your face is very familiar,
    but I have trouble with names"

Remembering names

92. Ushers who know the names of the people in the congregation and can remember the names of new people long enough to introduce them, have reached a high standard of excellence. To begin with, it is good to have in the ushers' desk a complete list of the church constituency by name, address, and phone number. There are many times when this information is needed by ushers. Since most people profess to difficulty in remembering names, there is a general feeling among ushers, "I just can't remember peoples names, only their faces." However, here are some helps:

(1) Create enough interest in a person to listen to his name until it is accurately understood in your own mind. Most people do not know the names of other persons because they do not listen. If necessary ask the individual to repeat his name, even to spell it.

(2) Relate the name to someone or something which has special meaning. The person's name may be the same as some special friend or relative. Or a name may be a reminder of a place or experience. Although many jokes have been told about confusion resulting from relating names to people, places and things, it still is an excellent tool in helping to remember.

(3) Use the person's name at least three times as soon as possible. Call the person by his name as you speak to him. Use the person's name while introducing him to someone else. Tell someone else about the person you have met, using his name.

(4) Write down the name. One traveling preacher who was noted for remembering thousands of names, used several techniques in his system of memory. However, one of the most important things he did was to write down the name in his notebook as soon as he was alone. After using a person's name several times and then writing it in his notebook, he found it much easier to remember. And in case of a memory lapse, he always had a ready reference.

Concentrating on the other individual

93. Although your time may be limited, concentrate fully on the visitor you are greeting. Look him or her in the eye, smile, shake hands warmly, and above all talk about him. Do not let everything he says to you remind you of something about yourself. Talk optimistically and happily about your own church. Think of good things you can say enthusiastically about your pastor and the people in your church, and let these things become a part of your conversation with all visitors.

Introducing people to each other

94. After greeting new people, try not to leave them standing alone at the end of your conversation. If possible, leave them in conversation with someone to whom you have introduced them. The more people a new person can meet in the church, the more possibilities there are for building bridges of understanding and fellowship which may be reason enough for making attendance at church more worthwhile. As far as possible, try to make these introductions with persons who may have some mutual interests. Young couples like to meet other young couples. Unmarried young people like to meet other unmarried young people. Men in business or the professions enjoy meeting other men in similar businesses or professions. Every time a new couple is introduced to someone else, they can hear the church say, "We are interested in you!" Introducing one person to another need not to be a threatening situation. There are just a few simple rules to remember:

(1) Begin an introduction by calling the name of the honored person. For instance, Dr. Famous, I want you to meet Mr. Lesser-known. Your pastor, visiting church dignitaries, older citizens and well-known persons are among those who are honored persons and therefore their name is mentioned first in an introduction.

(2) Always introduce lower priority people to higher

priority people. People of lower seniority, younger age, or lesser importance are always introduced to people of higher seniority, greater age or more importance. For instance:

"Mr. Older, I want to introduce you to Miss Younger."

"Mrs. Old-timer, I would like you to meet Mrs. New-comer."

"Rev. Dr., I want you to meet Miss Secretary."

(3) Use full names. It is not good etiquette to use either first names or last names by themselves in introductions. Informal warmth is a social grace in any church, but a lack of respect is not. Informal use of first names develops as friendship grows. But, the use of a person's last name without his first name and title is never a sign of respect. In regimented situations such as the army, last names are often used. But in the social graces which accompany a church service it is good to introduce people both by their titles and first and last names. There will be plenty of time later for the informalities.

Very important persons

95. On occasion there are visitors in the congregation whose presence should be known by the pastor. Some discreet communication system can be devised for keeping the pastor informed. A note from the ushers to the pastor at the time the collection is received is one of the most common means for this type of communication. Obviously, the pastor will use his own discretion in the public recognition of visitors.

Suggestions for Study and Training

1. Assign one of the men to read Matthew 9:2 - 8 on the four ushers who brought the paralytic to Christ.

2. For practice in remembering names, show the group a series of pictures from magazine advertisements of men, women and families. Explain a little about each one and introduce them by name. Test them later by showing the

pictures again to see how many names the men can remember. With practice their individual abilities to remember should increase.

3. Do role playing in introducing people according to suggestions indicated in paragraph #94.